DATE DUE

APR 13			
MAR 04			
OCT 26			

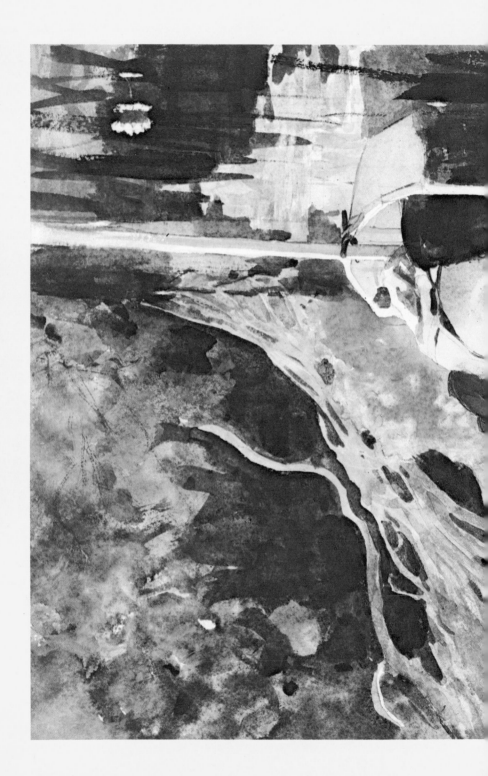

WINSLOW HOMER

America's Old Master

WINSLOW HOMER
America's Old Master

LINDA HYMAN

Winslow Homer

DOUBLEDAY & COMPANY, INC.

GARDEN CITY, NEW YORK

First Edition

ISBN: 0-385-03488-1 Trade
0-385-07823-4 Prebound
Library of Congress Catalog Card Number 72–92225
Copyright © 1973 by Linda Hyman
Printed in the United States of America

JB

Acknowledgments

I would like to acknowledge my indebtedness to the late Albert Ten Eyck Gardner, who introduced me to many of Winslow Homer's magnificent paintings. My gratitude is also extended to Lloyd Goodrich, Philip C. Beam and John Wilmerding for their inspiring works on this artist. I thank the members of the American Paintings Department of The Metropolitan Museum, who have been constantly helpful and supportive. My special thanks go to Peter Hyun, whose friendship, encouragement and professionalism have given me the incentive to begin and the courage to complete this book. And, finally, I am proud to have benefited so much during recent years from the love and support of my family and friends—especially my sister and Susan.

To my father

ILLUSTRATIONS

Black-and-White Illustrations

Color Illustrations

INTRODUCTION

Winslow Homer is one of America's best-known and well-loved artists. There are some experts today who think that Winslow Homer is, in fact, the very best artist that America has ever produced. He even achieved a great deal of fame and fortune during his own lifetime, which is something that doesn't always happen. And yet, strange as it may seem, this famous artist spent most of the last twenty-five years of his life living and painting alone, in a secluded house and studio, high on a cliff on the rocky coast of Maine. For days, weeks and sometimes months on end, Winslow Homer would be alone with the raging sea and only his little terrier, Sam, as a companion.

Why did Homer turn his back on the world and choose this difficult life? What kind of life did he lead before he moved to Maine—how did he pass his childhood and schooling in Boston, and his years as a young artist in the busy New York art world? We wonder what his family was like and what kind of things he enjoyed doing in his free time. But the most important question, of course, is what kind of pictures did he paint and why did he paint them.

If we can find out about an artist's life, and if we put this information together with a long careful look at his paintings, an interesting thing might result. That is, by knowing his life and his work, we can learn what the artist was like as a person. We can discover certain thoughts he had, some of his feelings, his hopes and desires, his likes and dislikes. In other words, we can get to know the artist's personality. And, instead of being just a name in a book or a signature on a painting, he almost comes to life. And then, if we are lucky, we will also see something about the world he lived in, and how he was a part of it or how he changed it. Learning about an artist and his work often leads us down new or forgotten roads, where we make all sorts of unexpected explorations and discoveries.

In this book we will go back over a hundred years in time to explore the fascinating life and work of one man, and see why he is called America's "Old Master" painter. This is the story of Winslow Homer, the man and the artist, and the America he lived in during the nineteenth century.

CHAPTER 1

"If a man wants to be an artist,
he should never look at pictures."

Winslow Homer was born in Boston, Massachusetts, on February 24, 1836. He was a Yankee in the true sense of the word, for the Homer family had been living in New England for many generations. The first Homer to come to America was Captain John Homer, the master of a ship trading between London and Boston. He settled in Massachusetts with his family during the 1600s. Following the lead of Captain John, many of Winslow Homer's ancestors continued as foreign traders. They were not an enormously rich family, but they did build a reputation as comfortable, respectable New England citizens.

Winslow's father, Charles Savage Homer, was a busy hardware merchant in Boston. His mother, Henrietta, came from the Benson family of Bucksport, Maine, but had grown up near Boston. Winslow had two brothers, Charlie who was older, and Arthur who was younger. When he was very young he developed an especially close and loving relationship with his older brother, Charlie. This special friendship lasted all of Winslow's life and, as we will see, created some interesting and amusing situations.

When Winslow was six his family moved across the Charles River to the nearby town of Cambridge. Their new house was on Massachusetts Avenue, very near Harvard College. At that time Cambridge was a small village with open, rolling countryside just beyond. The Homer boys enjoyed a happy country childhood, constantly roaming the hills and woods where they loved to swim, hunt and fish. This was one of the happiest periods of Winslow's life, a time he always looked back to with great pleasure. And, it developed in him his lifelong passion for a solitary, outdoor sporting life.

Winslow expressed his love for drawing at a very early age and, although it was unusual in those days, his parents did not try to discourage him. The few drawings that survive from his youth show us that Homer was an extraordinarily gifted child. Even at the age of ten his drawings show a clear, strong hand carefully at work observing surrounding scenes and objects. And in subject matter they reveal a young boy's feeling for a carefree, rural life. Three of his earliest works show pictures of a farmhouse, a hay wagon, and a drawing of a young boy dreaming in a meadow. Perhaps the last one, which he titled *Adolescence,* is a picture of Winslow's brother Charlie, drawn while the two boys were lazing away a summer afternoon in the countryside.

If it is true, as some people say, that artistic talent runs in the family, then Winslow's mother seems the obvious source of his gift. Henrietta Maria Homer had been well educated at a young ladies' school where she had been taught the rudiments of watercolor painting. Most well-bred young ladies of the time, in fact, were taught watercolor painting. It was one of the fashionable pastimes that occupied their idle hours before marriage. But Henrietta didn't stop painting when she married Mr. Homer. She painted delicate, detailed, careful studies of flowers, year after year, all her life. Occasionally she even exhibited her work in professional art shows. One show in Brooklyn in the 1870s had pictures by both Winslow

Homer and his mother. A cousin of Winslow's once said: "He got it all from his mother. She was always painting pictures. I went to see her *just* before Winslow was born, and she had on a big pinafore and was standing before a large easel painting."

Very different from most parents of the time, who thought art was not a "useful" pursuit, Homer's parents did not try to channel his interests in other directions. His mother, of course, must have been secretly proud that her son was following in her footsteps at such a young age. And his father, when on a business trip in London, sent young Winslow a complete set of anatomical prints—representations of heads, faces, hands, legs and other parts of the human body. Mr. Homer also sent prints of trees, houses, animals and other objects to teach the beginning draftsman. A friend of Homer's many years later reported that in the 1870s he still had "a pile of crayon reproductions of all sorts of things, made as early as 1847, each picture being supplemented with his full name and exact date in a careful juvenile fashion."

Charlie Homer had, as he later put it, "wriggled through Harvard College." But his brother Winslow, who had never been very interested in school, announced to his family that all he really wanted to do was draw pictures. His father wisely recognized Winslow's talent and interest, and decided not to push the idea of a college education. Instead, he spoke to his friend John Bufford, a well-known print maker, and arranged for Winslow to learn the trade of lithography in Bufford's big Boston shop. Bufford's, in fact, was one of the largest and most active shops of its kind in the country. They produced huge quantities of prints for posters, books, magazines, cards and sheet music. Winslow's first assignments were designing illustrations for covers of popular songs. He later joked about the rather sentimental pictures he drew for such songs as "Minnie Clyde," "Katy Darling" and "Annie Laurie."

But it didn't take old Mr. Bufford long to recognize that in Winslow Homer he had an apprentice of unusual ability. Soon he had Homer doing much more complicated pictures such as a large print of the entire Massachusetts Senate that included forty-eight separate portraits. Winslow, however, was not particularly flattered by such an important assignment. It took him many months to finish it and he considered this kind of painstaking work to be nothing but drudgery.

Among the young apprentices who worked with Homer at Bufford's were the future painters Joseph E. Baker and Joseph Foxcroft Cole. Years later, Baker remembered Homer as "short, delicately built, with a good figure, a shock of dark brown hair, hazel eyes, a little moustache, and a patchy beard. He carried himself very straight and used to work standing up, so as not to get round-shouldered. He displayed little emotion or change of expression; if Bufford did not like his work he never showed any feeling about it." Baker noticed right from the first that Homer was the cleverest in drawing and that he was already determined to be a great painter. During his first year of apprenticeship Homer said to his other friend, Joseph Cole: "If a man wants to be an artist, he should never look at pictures."

Homer worked at Bufford's shop six days a week, from eight in the morning until six at night. He desperately missed the happy outdoor life of his earlier years, especially in the summer. Sometimes he would get up at three in the morning and walk several miles to Fresh Pond. Here he would relax and fish and daydream awhile before getting on the horse-drawn trolley to go to work. Winslow hated the work at Bufford's, and when he reached the age of twenty-one he promptly quit, announcing to his friends and family that he would never again work for another man. He kept this promise faithfully for the rest of his life.

Homer began his life as an independent artist by doing illustrations. He started by doing a series of scenes illustrating everyday life in Boston for *Ballou's Pictorial Magazine.* He also began sending his pictures to *Harper's Weekly,* a new illustrated magazine based in New York. It didn't take Winslow Homer long to become one of *Harper's* best and most popular illustrators. These were the days before photography was developed for use in magazines, so publications were dependent on good artists like Homer to provide pictures. His drawings of college life at Harvard and activities in the country around Boston were particularly admired by the thousands of readers of *Harper's Weekly.* It was soon apparent that Homer's drawings stood out from all the others in the magazine. He had begun to develop a personal style of drawing which clearly set his work apart from that being done by other artists. His illustrations were fresher, more realistic and drawn with a much abler hand.

When Homer was twenty-four, in the fall of 1859, he decided to leave Boston and try to further his career in New York. New York had become the art and publishing center of the country, and Homer felt the need to live and work in these surroundings. He wanted to know other artists and be more a part of the active art scene that he had heard so much about. But Homer always thought of Boston as his home, and for many years he returned to spend part of each summer with his parents and brothers. Although he gained his first successes in New York and remained there to work for many years, he never felt completely at home there. When he finally left New York for good after twenty years, he returned to a simple, country life in his beloved New England.

CHAPTER 2

"A button on a barn door . . ."

When Homer arrived in New York he took a room in a boarding house belonging to Mrs. Alexander Cushman on East Sixteenth Street and rented a studio farther downtown on Nassau Street. He soon made friends with several of his fellow boarders, especially the Howland brothers: Alfred, a painter, and Henry, who later became a judge. A photograph taken of Homer and his friends at the time shows six young men, all with very serious expressions on their faces. Homer is wearing mutton-chop whiskers and long hair. We see what a closely knit group these young men were when we read a diary kept at the time by Alfred Howland. He sailed for France in June 1860 and wrote that his friends, including Winslow Homer, "went down the bay with me. . . . The band plays stirring pieces, and as we cross the bar, the fellows gather round me on the deck . . . and each presents me with a Yankee Doodle one cent, marked, so that I will be able to remember the giver. How I love these fellows! If they were only going with me, life would seem a perfect bliss."

Soon after Homer moved to New York he was offered a fabulous job as a staff artist for *Harper's Weekly*. "I declined it," he later said, "because I had had a taste of freedom. The slavery at Bufford's was too fresh in my recollection to let me care to bind myself again. From the time I took my nose off that lithographic stone, I have had no master; and never shall have any." Instead of working in an office as a staff artist, Homer became a free-lance illustrator and sold his pictures mainly to *Harper's Weekly* for the next seventeen years. He was never forced to illustrate a written story or article, but was free to make pictures of whatever subjects he thought were interesting or pleasing to the eye. During this phase of his career, Homer chose to illustrate people at work and at play in New York, New England and sometimes in the South.

One of the first pictures Homer did in New York for *Harper's* was the double-page Christmas drawing for 1859. This was soon followed by other pictures of the city in winter, one of the most charming being *Skating on the Ladies' Pond in Central Park, New York*. The description which accompanied the picture explained that in Central Park the lakes were divided into the Ladies' Pond and the Gentlemen's Pond. And it added that in the Ladies' Pond "no gentlemen are allowed to skate unless they are accompanied by ladies." Looking at this picture today, we wonder how those fashionable creatures actually managed to skate, all done up in their top hats, canes and billowy hoop skirts!

During these years Homer often visited the few art galleries that existed in New York. "What I remember best," he later told a friend, "is the smell of paint. I used to love it in a picture gallery." Twenty years later he remarked that he had been very much impressed with a picture he had seen in New York at the Dusseldorf Gallery. It was painted by William Page, who had just returned from a ten-year stay in Rome, and was entitled *Venus Rising from the Sea*. What Homer liked best in this picture was the rich and vibrant use of color and a special glazing technique Page had acquired in Venice, which was unknown in New York at that time.

In 1861, after living in the boarding house for two years, Homer moved to the New York University Building on Washington Square, where several of his fellow artists had studios. His own studio was in the tower room, at the top of a long flight of steep stairs. A door opened from the studio out onto a flat roof, where he often went to paint. He found it useful to pose models outdoors on the roof in order to get the proper effect of sunlight on the figures. The artists in this building had a visitor in 1866, who wrote: "We shall never be able to understand why eight or ten of these pleasant fellows have located themselves in the New York University. There isn't a more gloomy structure . . . ; and we hold that few men could pass a week in those lugubrious chambers without adding a morbid streak to their natures. . . . It has taken us some time to reach Mr. Homer's *atelier*, for it is on the third or fourth floor. But the half-finished picture on the easel, the two or three crayon sketches on the walls (military subjects), and the splendid view from his one window, cause us to forget that last long flight of stairs. The studio itself does not demand particular notice . . . it seems altogether too small for a man to have a large idea in." But Homer himself didn't seem to mind, and certainly the size of his ideas didn't seem to suffer! He stayed there for over ten years.

Winslow Homer first went to the South when the Civil War broke out. He was sent to the front lines several times to do illustrations for *Harper's Weekly*. In his war drawings he concentrated on the everyday life of the soldiers. He was more interested in life in camp than heroic or bloody battle scenes. These very realistic drawings revealed a sense of honesty and character that soon made Homer famous.

It has been said that no other artist left so authentic a record of how the Civil War soldier really looked and acted.

But Homer was not satisfied with his career as an illustrator. He wanted to be a painter. He began night classes in painting at the National Academy of Design and took four or five lessons with Frederic Rondel, a French painter living in New York. Aside from these few formal lessons, Homer was basically self-taught. At twenty-six he began painting seriously. His earliest works were of the Civil War. "His first picture in oils," wrote Russell Shurtleff, a landscape painter who knew Homer in those days, "was painted in his studio in the old University Building in Washington Square. It represented a 'Sharpshooter' seated in a brig top, aiming at a distant 'Reb,' a canvas about 16 by 20. I sat with him many days while he worked on it, and remember discussing with him how much he could ask for it. He decided not less than sixty dollars, as that was what Harper paid him for a full-page drawing on the wood." At about the same time Homer did another oil, of a soldier being punished for drunkenness by being made to stand on a barrel with a log over his shoulder. He commented on this painting many years later, telling a friend, "It is about as beautiful as a button on a barn door." Like most other artists, Homer was not especially proud of his first attempts at oil painting.

Two of Homer's earliest paintings were exhibited at the National Academy of Design. He told his family and friends that this was his way of testing the public's reaction to his work. He swore that if the two pictures did not sell he would simply give up painting for good. But Winslow's brother Charlie, who had great faith in Homer and did not want him to stop painting, decided to take no chances with the public. The two works were quickly bought by an "anonymous collector." What Winslow did not know until many

years later was that the nameless buyer of his first two paintings was none other than his brother Charlie!

Homer's great masterpiece from the Civil War period is
Prisoners from the Front. In this picture we see a Union
officer confronting a small group of Confederate prisoners.
They are standing in the midst of the war-torn, sadly dev-
astated Virginia countryside. The contrast between the
ragged, dejected prisoners and the haughty, well-groomed
officer is very moving and dramatic. Each face in the painting is a fine delineation of character and personality, particularly that of the old man. The great success of this picture
lies in the point of view taken by the artist, who seems to
understand the meaning of the Civil War from both sides of
the conflict. *Prisoners from the Front* is a statement of the
victory of the North, but at the same time it understands and
sympathizes with the temperament of the proud, though
beaten, Confederate Army. Homer's ability to perceive and
portray his subjects in a straightforward, honest manner is
one of the most important features of his art. This painting
was an immediate sensation in New York and solidly estab-
lished Homer's reputation as a first-rate artist. From this point
on, Winslow Homer was never obscure.

When not occupied with war assignments, Homer devoted
himself to oil painting. He had several favorite themes,
certain special subjects that he painted again and again, but
always in a slightly different way. In many of these pictures
we see children playing a leading role. Although Homer
never married and had no children, he always loved and
understood young people. It has been said that he often
painted the world as a young boy would feel and see it, the
only difference being that he painted it with a grown man's
"grasp of actuality." One of his best-known paintings of
children is called *Snap the Whip* and shows a group of

PRISONERS FROM THE FRONT
The Metropolitan Museum of Art
Gift of Mrs. Frank B. Potter, 1922

HIGH TIDE: THE BATHERS

The Metropolitan Museum of Art

Gift of Mrs. William F. Milton, 1923

happy boys playing a game in their schoolyard during recess. The sunlit New England meadow, the enthusiasm of the running children and the little red schoolhouse in the background capture an especially delightful moment from America's past. Paintings like *Snap the Whip* have become pictorial documents of our country's history.

Another of Homer's favorite themes of this period was the world of popular summer resorts. From Mount Washington in New Hampshire to Long Branch in New Jersey, with many stops in between, Homer carefully sketched and painted scenes of people riding on horseback, playing croquet, picnicking and swimming. Most of the people in these scenes are women and girls. They are pictured as healthy, happy young ladies with brightly colored hoop skirts, ribbons and sunbonnets. Homer delighted in these beautiful, young creatures and loved to paint their colorful costumes against the bright green grass and clear blue sky. In one such scene, done at Long Branch, we see a group of such girls gathered on a dune. We can almost feel the fresh sea breeze as it gently blows their flounced skirts and parasols. In another picture, *High Tide,* the girls appear on a beach, having just come out of the water in their dripping, clinging bathing costumes. In those days, swimming at the beach was still considered by some people as not entirely proper for nice young ladies. One art critic, discussing this picture in a newspaper article, declared that it was "perhaps not quite refined."

Most of the critics, in fact, found Homer's art at this time to be quite radical. He was one of the first American artists to paint scenes and people exactly as he saw them—he never tried to idealize them or make them more attractive than they actually were. This approach was certainly a giant departure from the artistic tradition. The critics commented that Homer preferred to paint "homely" subjects, that his colors were sometimes "peculiar," and they could not understand why some of his paintings seemed to be "unfinished."

The public, on the other hand, adored Homer's work from the start. In it they recognized scenes from a way of life they knew and loved. Most other art of the period pictured faraway places or illustrations from history and mythology. From the very beginning, although modestly at first, Homer always found a good market for his pictures. They usually sold quickly and, as the years passed, for higher and higher prices. Winslow Homer, unlike many artists, never had to worry about money.

In the fall of 1866, when he was thirty years old, Homer went to Paris and stayed for ten months. We know very little about what he did during his stay. But we do know that he visited the great world's fair, the Universal Exposition of 1867, where his famous Civil War picture, *Prisoners from the Front,* was on exhibition. We also know that he visited Paris' great art museum, the Louvre. But there is no record of whether he met any of the French Impressionist painters who were working in Paris at that time. Homer most likely went his own way, not caring to study or be influenced by other men's work. As has been said, "Homer looked more at nature than at other men's art, painted by eye rather than by tradition."

Homer's style at this time, as in later years, was entirely individualistic. He was one of the first American painters to leave the studio and work outdoors. He was interested in the special effects of light and color only as they can be seen out of doors. Although the things he painted were always important to him, equally important were the many different effects of light as it fell on those things. Homer also had a special feeling for painting as a form of decoration. He realized that lines, shapes and colors, as well as depicting specific things, can also be beautiful by themselves. His style was always basically realistic, but at the same time Homer liked to create abstract patterns with his lines, shapes and colors. This decorative quality in his paintings closely resembles similar qualities in Japanese art. And, in fact, Homer may possibly have been directly influenced by Japanese art, for his friend, a painter named John La Farge, was one of America's first collectors of Japanese prints. It is very probable that Homer saw some of these prints and that they made a strong impression on him.

In 1880, another of Homer's paintings, *Camp Fire,* became a huge public success. It was perhaps at this point that the artist started to think seriously about what artistic direction to take in the future. His pictures up to this time illustrated a wide variety of subjects, which usually were pleasantly portrayed, but never investigated very deeply. Homer had become a very able professional painter, a very talented artist with a firm reputation. He was, however, still not satisfied. He began to realize that he was not yet a serious thinker or a painter of deeply meaningful pictures. It was now time to search for something—a feeling, an idea, an experience—something that would help him take the next step forward with his art. A seed of genius already existed within the artist, but it was something that had to be developed further. And to do so, Homer decided that it was now necessary to leave the world of busy cities and gay seaside resorts. He decided to leave his friends and family behind and spend some time working and thinking in solitude. This way he hoped to be able to develop his art by experimenting with new subjects and new forms.

In 1881, Homer again left America, but this time he did

not go to Paris. Instead, he chose to stay in England, in the small seaport called Tynemouth on the North Sea. Homer's two-year stay here became the real turning point of his life and his art.

CHAPTER 3

"Nowhere on our coasts are storms
more frequent or more terrible."

No one knows why Winslow Homer decided to go to England, and certainly his reasons for choosing Tynemouth are still a mystery. Tynemouth at that time was a crowded seaport of forty-four thousand people. It was a popular summer resort as well as the home of the great North Sea fishing fleet. When Homer arrived he was immediately faced with the sights and sounds of the noisy factories and barges and all the activities of this busy coastal city. As much as Homer was drawn to all this, he also loved the peace and quiet of the countryside. So he rented a small house in the nearby suburb of Cullercoates. The house had a lovely garden and was surrounded by a high wall that provided the privacy the artist wanted. Here he lived and worked for two years, even doing his own cleaning and cooking. Every day Homer would walk into Tynemouth and spend many hours making sketch after sketch of the fascinating sights he encountered. And soon he discovered that something strange was happening to him.

It seemed that Winslow Homer's taste was changing. The same subjects that he had happily painted for many years no longer appealed to him. The carefree colorful life of the seaside resort did not fascinate or even amuse him any more.

Even the pretty young girls and the sunbathers on the beach
failed to arouse his interest. The elements of artistic genius
that had begun to take shape in Homer could no longer
be satisfied by such artificial activity. He needed to paint
something more substantial, something more meaningful, and
fortunately he was able to fulfill this need in Tynemouth.
Homer found his new inspiration through his fascination
with the Tynemouth weather and his interest in the local
fisherfolk. As before, he was still responding directly to his
surroundings. But this time his response was more mature
and more thoughtful.

Soon after he arrived in Tynemouth, Homer was struck
by the extreme difference in nature. It was a rainy and
stormy place with a heavy, wet atmosphere. But sometimes
the brilliant sun would break through heavy rain clouds and
create spectacular effects on the sea. The contrasts in color
and brilliance and the ever-present mist that seemed to make
everything shimmer were enormously appealing to Homer.
He began to paint magnificent studies of the mist, fog and
clouds, and of the changing effects of light on the sea. He
also was attracted by the frightening power of the sudden
storms and gales, and began to paint studies of the thundering waves as they rolled in from the sea and broke on the
shore. Homer would no doubt have agreed with an English
writer who said of Tynemouth in 1883: "Nowhere on our
coasts are storms more frequent or more terrible."

Homer's new sensitivity to climate and weather brought
about some major changes in his art. In his earlier pictures,
weather had always been seen as something static or un-
changing. Now it was painted as a dynamic or constantly
moving force. The sea was no longer a quiet expanse of
water—it became a changing pattern of moving waves and
swells. And the sky was no longer a uniform area of brilliant

blue—it developed into a constantly shifting spectacle of cloud formations seen through changing forms of light and mist. We see that here in Tynemouth Homer found himself in a much closer relationship with the weather. He was responding directly to the dramatic and ever-changing moods of nature.

Turning away from the summer resort activities, Homer soon found a new and deeper inspiration in the lives of the fishing community. By studying these people, Homer was able to see how closely their lives were connected with nature. These were people who made their living directly from the sea, not people who simply played on the edge of the sea. They were sturdy, hard working and immediately gained the artist's admiration and respect. For the first time Homer understood the effects of nature on men, the closeness between the sea and the people of the sea. Homer was deeply impressed. This is seen clearly in his work done at Tynemouth. He later said that he sketched and painted these people day and night and worked harder than he ever had before. He had also never stayed in one place for so long to paint.

Women became a major theme of Homer's Tynemouth paintings, but they were nothing like any women he had painted before. In his American scenes he had painted fashionable young ladies—he pictured them as delightful creatures, dainty figures decorating pleasant scenes. But the Tynemouth women were a new type to Homer, who saw them as sturdy, strong, serious people, capable of doing men's work. He painted them as they worked, or in the boats or as they looked out to sea. In many scenes Homer caught something of the haunting, almost desperate quality of these strong-minded women, as they quietly waited and watched for the safe return of their men. In fact, women are portrayed

much more often in these pictures than men. But through
the activities and expressions of the women we are also able
to understand the lives of the men.

Homer viewed the people of Tynemouth not so much as
separate individuals but as part of a working community.
The beach was the center of activity for these fishing families.
When the fleet came in at night, every boat was filled to the
brim with fish. The exhausted men would go right home,
and then the women's work would begin. They unloaded the
fish, prepared it for the market and were in charge of selling
it at the market. Afterward they returned to the boats to
clean them and restock them with food and supplies. They
cleaned and repaired the fishing tackle and gear and got the
ship ready for its early morning departure. Then they would
talk and gossip while they again patiently waited for their
men to return safely at night. The danger of their men
getting caught in a storm was always present, and it created
a certain tenseness among the people onshore.

In Homer's best Tynemouth pictures he has clearly shown
the close relationship between the people and the sea. Some
of his most spectacular scenes show the reaction of the fishing
community during violent storms. In *Watching the Tempest*
we see a rescue crew lined up next to their lifeboat, alert
and ready to launch it the moment it is needed. At the right
we see some women nervously looking around the bow of the
boat. In the distance a crowd of anxious people are lined up
along a cliff, and high above the whole scene is the Coast
Guard Station. Everything in this picture tells us of the
tension and strain these people must live through every time
there is a storm at sea.

Homer devoted a good deal of time in Tynemouth to
painting and sketching in water color. He had often tried
water colors in America, but it was in England that he really

Eight Bells

Addison Gallery of American Art
Phillips Academy, Andover, Massachusetts

WATCHING THE TEMPEST

Courtesy of the Fogg Art Museum, Harvard University

Grenville L. Winthrop Bequest

was able to develop and master the technique. With this
new mastery, the figures that he painted lost their former
traces of stiffness, becoming more flexible and mobile. They
also became larger and rounder, seeming to move more
freely in the space of the picture. As Homer's mastery of
the water-color technique began to take hold, we see that
his work grew from simple colored drawings to full-fledged,
fully-developed water-color paintings. The thinness of paint
of his earlier water colors disappeared, and a new strength
and fullness were obtained through the use of washes. He
now learned how to get different varieties of white—before
he had simply left portions of the white paper unpainted, but
now he discovered how to "lift" colors off the paper with a
wet brush or scrape colors off with a knife.

Homer painted his water colors "on the spot," usually as
he sat near the scene he was trying to capture. He repeated
many of the themes over and over, trying to develop and
master the water-color medium. Often he would sketch the
same scene or people from several different angles or in
different lights. We see from the titles of these works that
no matter what the artist was painting, he was never very
far from the fishing community. *Mending the Nets, The
Incoming Tide, A Voice from the Cliffs* and *A Scotch Mist*
are among his most successful water colors of Tynemouth.

Homer exhibited four of his best English water colors at
the American Water Color Society in 1883. The public was
more enthusiastic than ever, and even the most hesitant of
the art critics seem to have been finally won over with this
show. In a review of Homer's work in *Century Magazine,*
the art critic Margaret Van Rensselaer said: " 'The Voice
from the Cliffs' and 'Inside the Bar' seem to me not only the
most complete and beautiful things he has yet produced, but
among the most interesting American art has yet created.

INSIDE THE BAR, TYNEMOUTH
The Metropolitan Museum of Art
Gift of Louise Ryals Arkell, 1954, in memory of her husband, Bartlett Arkell

. . . The dignity of these landscapes and the sturdy vigor of these figures, translated by the strong sincerity of his brush, prove an originality of mood, a vigor of conception, and a sort of stern poetry of feeling. . . ."

The two years Winslow Homer spent in Tynemouth have been called the real turning point of his life. It was the period in which he grew from youth to maturity. It was the time when the seeds of genius really began to flower in his art. Before he went to Tynemouth, Homer had seen only a few of the different sides of nature and had hardly begun to understand the depths of his fellow men. He had seen some of the Civil War, but he was still very young. For the most part, his world had been pleasant, gay, charming and beautiful. It was only at Tynemouth that Homer began to see other, more serious sides of human life, and these made a great impression on him. From this point on, Homer was to become a more serious and thoughtful person himself.

Perhaps the most important aspect of Homer's experience at Tynemouth is that it brought him into close contact with the sea. He grew to love the sea at Tynemouth, to almost feel a living part of it himself. And certainly it was his deep-felt response to the sea and its people that brought about some major changes in Homer's life and art. First of all, it prompted him to decide to live close to the sea for the rest of his life. And second, it settled in his mind the kind of pictures he wanted to paint in the future. And finally, it was probably at Tynemouth that Homer decided to live alone for the rest of his life, for he learned that this was the way he worked the best.

Homer, in fact, was not the only artist in the second half of the nineteenth century who preferred to live and work in voluntary solitude. There were Gauguin (in Tahiti), Cézanne (in the South of France) and Van Gogh (in Holland). These men were all probably reacting to similar situations in the world and in society. The beginnings of industrialization, the rapid growth of big cities, the migration of country people to urban centers, the faster moving pace of life, the flowering of technological and scientific discoveries—all these led to feelings of confusion and the unwillingness on the part of some people to cope with the complexities and frustrations of modern society. Toward the end of the nineteenth century there was a self-imposed move back to a more basic, natural way of life, especially among men of artistic temperaments. Like Homer, these men found it necessary to have a more direct relationship with nature in order to develop their genius and create great art.

Homer had gone to England in order to find a new direction for his life and art. It took two years in Tynemouth for him to realize that a solitary life by the sea was to be his final and logical solution. This was the last step he must take in order to achieve the kind of greatness he was looking for. Once Homer realized this, there was really no further reason for him to stay in England. America was, after all, his home. So, in the fall of 1882, Homer boarded the ocean liner *Catalonia* and headed back to America. When he entered New York Harbor in November, he was ready to make that last move, and he knew exactly where he had to go and what he had to do.

CHAPTER 4

"Oh hear us when we cry to Thee,
For those in peril on the sea."

Homer returned for a short time to his old studio in New York, but he soon discovered that New York no longer had what he needed. In Tynemouth he had developed a certain relationship with the sea, the cold, clean air, and the special people who lived by the ocean. None of these existed in New York, and Homer found he could not paint without them. What he needed, in fact, was an American version of Tynemouth, and he thought he knew just where to find it. About eight years earlier Homer had visited his brother Arthur during his honeymoon in Maine. It was a majestic and secluded place on the coast, about twelve miles south of Portland, on Saco Bay. Homer remembered it well. The name of the place was Prout's Neck, and it was exactly what he was looking for. Before the spring was over Winslow Homer made the last and most important move of his life. Winslow, his father and his two brothers decided to settle at Prout's Neck.

The Homer family built a large house at Prout's Neck and called it "The Ark." They offered to build a studio for Winslow in The Ark, but the artist insisted on living alone. So he hired an architect and remodeled a nearby stable into a studio home. He built a large covered porch on the second floor which looked onto a wide expanse of sea and coast. So many hours were spent walking back and forth here and observing the sea that his brothers accused Winslow of "wearing out the balcony." High on a cliff, with a magnificent view of the sea, this home is where Homer stayed for the rest of his life. For the next twenty-five years, although he would often take trips to Canada or to the South, Homer always returned with pleasure to his life and work at Prout's Neck.

Homer's family, like a large proportion of people at Prout's Neck, were part of the summer colony. When the summer people were there the place was bustling with activity—clambakes, fishing excursions, picnics and children swimming and playing on the beach. During the summers, Homer occasionally joined his family for dinner in The Ark. But usually, even in summer, he could be found alone, walking the cliffs along the sea or working in his studio. And Homer would always stay on in Prout's Neck long after the summer people had gone, for fall and winter in Maine were especially pleasing to him. During these cold, dreary months, Homer still continued his long walks by the sea, always delighting in the waves, the weather and his own solitude. Although his closest neighbor was often many miles away, Homer always found peace and happiness alone with the sea.

The sea at Prout's Neck was a constantly changing, breathtakingly magnificent spectacle, particularly during the months of November and December. Homer took special pleasure in the more violent, raging storms, and sometimes stayed outside for hours in the cold and wet during a storm so he could study the wind and waves. A three-day north-easter, for instance, created fifty-foot waves that would break and send salt spray flying over the sixty-foot cliffs.

Sometimes, if the wind shifted to the west, it blew long streamers of water (called mare's-tails) from the tops of the big breakers. Standing in the midst of a howling autumn wind, Homer loved to watch the fast-moving clouds and listen to the pounding surf. He never failed to be amazed by these extraordinary displays of nature's power and beauty. But he also loved the quieter, more serene moments at Prout's Neck. He would often take long tranquil walks through the woods and rolling pastures, stopping to sketch interesting rock formations, sand dunes or marshes. Homer grew to know and love every inch of Prout's Neck. It was truly a painter's paradise.

Some years Homer stayed at the Neck for the entire winter often absolutely alone for days on end. But this way of life was one he had chosen for himself, and we see from his letters that he never seemed to suffer from loneliness or depression. On the contrary, the fewer people Homer had around him, the happier he seemed to be and the better he seemed to work. Late one September he wrote to his brother Charlie: "I like my home more than ever as people thin out." It is doubtful that Homer ever felt really alone at Prout's Neck. He was, after all, in extremely close contact with the elements of nature he loved the most. His deeply emotional relationship with nature probably replaced the need for such a relationship with his fellow men and kept him from feeling lonely. He told Charlie how much he loved Prout's Neck, saying, "The sun will not rise or set without my notice, and thanks."

Homer's thanks were expressed in his magnificent seascapes, results of endless and intense looking and feeling. These are products of a contemplative mind that spent many hours meditating on the beauty of nature that flooded through his eyes. They also reveal a truly artistic genius,

NORTHEASTER

The Metropolitan Museum of Art

Gift of George A. Hearn, 1910

finally able to translate the feelings in his heart into paint
on a canvas. Homer always remained faithful to actual life
and nature, taking great care to portray realistically everything he saw. At the same time, he was faithful to the
feelings in his heart and used nature as a means of accurately
expressing his feelings.

For several years after he moved to Maine, Homer's
principal pictures dealt with the perils of the sea. He had
spent part of the summer of 1883 in Atlantic City, New
Jersey, where he became interested in various lifesaving
techniques. One such technique, which used something called
a breeches buoy to rescue people from wrecks, was demon-
strated by some friends who were in a lifesaving crew. A few
months later, back at Prout's Neck, Homer used these re-
searches in an oil painting called *The Life Line*. In this
picture we see a coastguardman holding an unconscious
woman. Both of them are being pulled to shore with the
help of a breeches buoy. Far away in the background we see
a suggestion of the rocks and cliffs at Prout's Neck. And
in the upper left a wind-blown sail tells us of the presence
of a sailboat that has been dashed upon some rocks and is
about to break apart. The life line has been carried from
a cliff to the doomed ship and is pulled tightly but danger-
ously above the thundering waves.

Called by many critics Homer's first great masterpiece,
The Life Line is certainly his most dramatic painting so far.
In viewing this picture, we feel a real concern for the woman
and her rescuer as we sense their danger. We also have a
sense of man's strength and bravery when he comes to the
rescue of his fellow men. Man's basic heroic qualities are
clearly seen by the artist and are also appreciated by the
viewer of the painting. Homer has developed in this picture
the underlying theme that had originally captured his in-

THE LIFE LINE
The Philadelphia Museum of Art
The George W. Elkins Collection

terest at Tynemouth—the eternal battle for survival between man and nature. But in the Tynemouth paintings the actual danger of calamity at sea was merely referred to by the activities of the people on shore. In *The Life Line,* for the first time, we see the actual drama unfold before our eyes.

What is it about his picture that has caused so many people to call it a masterpiece? Certainly one answer is the dramatic force of the subject matter—we are drawn into the action much as if we were being involved in a play or movie. This drama is made more effective by the artist's style of painting. He paints the waves in a series of repeating lines and forms that create a certain pictorial rhythm. This pictorial or stylistic device almost makes us feel and hear the powerfully pounding rhythm of the breakers themselves. But the focus of our eyes is always led to the main action, the two figures being hauled by the life line. This is achieved through the use of another pictorial device—a diagonal line (formed by the waves) that leads our eye directly from the lower left into the center of the picture. This same line not only centers our attention in the appropriate place, it also creates a sense of depth or space in the picture by taking us from the foreground (the picture surface) into the middle ground (the picture space). Our attention is further focused on the unfortunate woman by an especially clever and realistic touch—the artist has chosen to cover the face of the rescuer with a wind-blown scarf, so that we only see the face of the woman. Perhaps the most effective element of Homer's style in developing the drama of this scene is the way he manipulates his paintbrush. Much of the force or violence felt in this picture comes from the forceful, vigorous vitality of the brushwork itself.

The model for the figure of the man in *The Life Line* was Henry Lee, a handyman who did odd jobs around

Homer's studio. He continued to pose for Homer for many years and for each day's modeling was rewarded with a five-dollar gold piece. Homer was friendly with many of the local people who lived and worked at Prout's Neck. In addition to Henry Lee, Homer made friends with Miss Hamilton, the elder Homer's housekeeper, with Elbridge Oliver, the station-master, and with Harris Seavey, the stagecoach driver and mail carrier. Another friend was Alvin Brown who owned a fish house on the beach on the west side of the Neck.

Homer's next great oil painting was *The Fog Warning,* in 1885. Working out his idea for the picture on the beach in front of Alvin Brown's fish house, he first piled up some sand to substitute for a wave. Then he propped up a dory against the sand pile and placed Henry Lee inside the boat to pose as a fisherman. In order to achieve a realistic effect, Homer even went so far as to dress poor Henry in oilskins and then douse him with a bucket of cold water! The first sketches were done on the spot in water color, but it took Homer many months of hard work to complete the final oil painting. In this picture we see a dory fisherman who is far away from his ship, the large schooner on the horizon. The fisherman has noticed the threatening gray clouds that are approaching, and he is quickly pulling in his fishing lines and preparing to row back to his ship. Once again Homer has painted a tense and dramatic event, another episode in the continuing battle between men and the sea. The longer we study this picture, the more we actually feel the uncertainty and suspense of the moment. If the fisherman is lucky, he will make it back to the schooner. If not, his tiny boat will be swamped by the immense waves, throwing him overboard to a cold and lonely death. As in *The Life Line,* Homer has been able to tell a story with a paintbrush. He has chosen, in both paintings, the moment of greatest danger,

THE FOG WARNING
Courtesy, Museum of Fine Arts, Boston
Otis Norcross Fund

so that the viewer becomes almost totally involved. And the outcome, or the final chapter of the story, is left entirely to the viewer's imagination.

During Homer's trip to England he had become fascinated with the art of navigating a ship. One thing that particularly interested him was the process of "shooting" the sun with a sextant in order to establish the ship's position. Several years later he bought a similar device, an octant, and kept it in his studio. One day in 1886 he posed Henry Lee and a neighbor, John Gatchell, with the octant, and began to paint rapidly and intensely. He finished the painting in just a few days, and the result of this inspiration is one of Homer's best pictures of men at sea, *Eight Bells*. Here again we are presented with a story, but the moment of greatest danger has passed. In this painting, the suspense and drama exist beneath the surface. Here we see two seamen, still in their oilskins, taking a reading on the ship's position. The sea and the sky, with the sun just beginning to break through the clouds, tell us that an enormous storm has recently ended. We can only wonder at the tremendous battle that has just taken place between these heroic men and the raging sea. And it is with a great sigh of relief that we notice the ending of the storm and the men resuming their duties.

All these pictures of men at sea have been called masterpieces. The main feature that they share is that they all bring forth emotions within us. Whether we feel worry, alarm, fear, admiration, happiness, sadness, calmness or relief—the one thing a masterpiece always does is make us *feel* something. Homer's series of dramatic scenes, done at Prout's Neck in the 1880s, all deal with the struggle between man and nature and the feelings and emotions that result from that struggle. These are simple, unsentimental feelings, typical of the earnest New Englanders of a century ago. And these brave people expressed the same depth or tone of feeling in the same straightforward manner in an old hymn of the sea. We can almost hear Winslow Homer as he joined the local folks in song at the small Prout's Neck church: "Oh hear us when we cry to Thee, For those in peril on the sea."

CHAPTER 5

"The only companion I want
is a Bobolink."

May 4, 1890
Dear Father:
Your rhubarb is up two feet although it was not
uncovered. But it came taking with it anything in the
way, three-inch plank, wheelbarrow, old wash tubs, and
whatever was over it, as seen from my window.

W.——

Winslow enjoyed a very close relationship with his father,
particularly after his mother died in the early 1880s. "Old
Father Homer," as he was called by the people at Prout's
Neck, was commonly known as a "character." He was, to
say the least, extremely property conscious, and was always
busy buying and selling land at Prout's Neck. At the same
time, he was always getting into fights about land. Even
after he sold a piece of property, he somehow thought he
still owned it and would often go around knocking down
fences with his cane. Father Homer was also known for his
odd habit of taking cold baths as a health remedy. A food
faddist who let his hair grow long, Mr. Homer must have
been quite an unusual sight to the summer people at Prout's
Neck. Winslow adored his father and would often kid him in

a well-meaning way. He had a habit of drawing amusing caricatures of his father and sending them to his brother Charles. And once he happily wrote Charles that "Father is having a good time by not agreeing to mind his own business and retire from active life."

During the 1890s, after the old man passed his eightieth birthday, Winslow took special care of him. Even though Winslow stayed in Maine during the winters, he would travel to Boston every two or three weeks to visit his father. In December 1895, he wrote to Charles's wife, Mattie: "Father and self have had a very pleasant Christmas. I shall go home tomorrow. I find that living with Father for three days, I grow to be so much like him that I am frightened. We get as much alike as two peas, in age and manners. He is very well, only he will starve himself. I shall go to Boston once in two weeks this next month to give him a dinner."

Of all the people he knew, Homer always remained closest to his brother Charlie. They grew even more intimate as the years went by, often traveling together and always exchanging letters. Charlie lived in New York, where he had become a successful chemist and rich businessman and an active member of society. But no matter how busy he was, his love for his family and his interest in his brother's art always came first. Whenever Winslow sent a finished painting down from Prout's Neck to his dealer in New York, Charlie would drop everything and run to the gallery to see it. He was intensely proud of his brother's growing reputation.

The special warmth of feeling that Winslow had for his brother also included Charlie's wife, Mattie. Mattie was known for her beauty, charm and intelligence, and was especially famous for her delightful dinner parties. We can see just how deeply Winslow felt about this couple in a letter he wrote to Arthur in June 1891, after seeing Charlie and

Mattie off to Europe: "I thought that you would all be glad to hear that Charlie and Mattie have had a fine day and the best steamer in the world to start them on their journey. Considering the old tubs that I have been over the ocean in, there is no doubt that they will have a fine voyage. I have never seen anyone off that I cared anything about and I found it hard, and I was glad when the steamer was off, but N.Y. seems empty now to me."

Except for occasional trips, Winslow spent most of every year in Prout's Neck. It is hard for us to imagine the difficulties of those cold and lonely winters in Maine, but we do see occasional mentions of the weather conditions in Winslow's letters: "The wind has been blowing so hard that I could not think of writing." "I do not keep a horse and my nearest neighbor is half a mile away—I am four miles from telegram and P.O. and under a snow bank most of the time." "These are tough days. Very cold; deep snow." In December 1890, he wrote to Charles: "I am getting in my ice—seven inches thick and clear as glass. My pond is quite different from what you think. The water all comes in from the bottom and runs off at the top. It's a pretty sight to see it now. . . . Thursday morning. The most beautiful day of the winter."

Despite all the difficulties, Homer managed to live quite well at Prout's Neck. He did most of his own cooking, using groceries and provisions that he ordered from Boston each week. Winslow's letters were often full of detailed talk about food, and from them we see that he was an excellent cook and enjoyed fine food. He wrote to Charles one spring: "I brought down Leg of Canada Mutton, two Spring Chickens, Bermuda onions, six bottles old rum, one Edam cheese, six bottles of rare old vatted whiskey, 'good as the Bank of England.' . . ." After a trip to Boston, Winslow wrote his father: "When I got home about one o'clock I opened my fish and cooked two shad roes and cut up a cucumber in cold water—then, with a quart of South Side Scarboro cider, I knew I was again in my own house."

Like most people who live alone, Homer enjoyed a few eccentricities or peculiarities. One example was his tendency to buy things he liked in large numbers. He always bought socks by the gross. When his brother tried to point out that this was foolish, Homer quickly answered: "When will you learn that the time to buy a thing is when you find what you want?"

Even more peculiar was the episode of the kerosene stoves, an amusing story that Charlie loved to tell and retell. It seemed that one day Charlie admired a new kerosene stove in Winslow's studio. He was immediately ushered out to the shed and was shown five more stoves just like it, still packed in their crates. "When I find something I really like, and wear it out, all too often I go back for another and discover it is no longer manufactured. Besides," Winslow added with a big smile, "these were a lot cheaper by the half dozen."

Winslow took great care of his appearance and paid attention to all the little details of his dress. When he made his rare social visits or appeared at other events, he always wore a high collar, a derby hat and a flower in his buttonhole. His thin build, straight posture, bald head, carefully trimmed mustache and steady gaze all combined to make a very impressive appearance. But Homer's looks did not resemble in the least the popular idea or image of an artist. A friend once remarked that "To look at him one could not imagine him painting." And a museum director who met Homer in 1896 wrote: "He was polite, modest, simple, without side. . . . Here was the essence of gentlemanly elegance. . . . He might have been taken for a successful stock-broker."

When he was not busy painting or walking, Homer could often be found working in his garden. He grew his own vegetables and was especially fond of his fresh corn. Once he decided to raise tobacco, and even went to a factory in Portland where he was taught how to roll his own cigars. The experiment, however, was never repeated, so we can imagine the quality of those cigars! More successful were Winslow's flowers, which he carefully tended every season. He loved the bright colors, shapes and smells of the flowers, and enjoyed arranging bouquets. Whenever Homer paid a visit to a friend or neighbor, he always offered his respects with a bouquet from his own garden. One neighbor remem-bered with a smile the sight of Homer walking two miles over the bluffs to pay a special visit—all dressed up in his most elegant clothes with a bouquet in one hand and a glass of imported sherry wine in the other!

For many years Homer's constant companion was his fox terrier, Sam. "After storms," wrote a friend, "we were sure of meeting the two walking along the paths and hunting the best surf, as we ourselves were doing, and Mr. Homer always stopped for us to talk to Sam. . . . The two always walked over to the post office at sunset for the mail, and it was really touching to see Mr. Homer walk so that Sam, growing more and more like a prize white pig and puffing so dreadfully, could keep up with him." Homer adored his pet, but after Sam died he refused to get another dog because he was afraid of getting too attached to it. After Sam's death he wrote to Charlie: "On *no* account send me a dog. The only companion I want is a Bobolink and the next time I go to Boston I shall get one. My rooms are very sunny this time of year, the sun being low shines under my top piazza into my house and with my new stove makes this place perfect—all but the Bobolink."

Odd jobs and outdoor activities kept Homer busy around the Neck. He had work to do on the land, building walls and roads, and in general taking care of his family's property during the absence of his father and brothers. Winslow seemed to like all this activity, as we see in a letter to Charlie in March 1896: "I am in receipt of your invitation to visit New York. It is too soon. I have things to do here that interest me more. I have just returned from burning brush over on the eastern Point."

The picture we get of Winslow Homer from his letters is hardly that of the embittered old hermit described by so many writers. Instead, we see a man who was perfectly content with his chosen way of life. In fact, Winslow Homer seemed to thoroughly enjoy his life, relishing every moment of activity—not only his painting, but all his outdoor activities, his cooking and his housekeeping. And even during the coldest, most difficult months, we never see any complaints or regrets. Homer always took delight in every aspect of nature and was altogether comfortable with his surroundings.

Winslow Homer wrote to his old friend Louis Prang in December 1893: "I deny that I am a recluse as is generally understood by that term. Neither am I an unsociable hog. . . . This is the only life in which I am permitted to mind my own business. I suppose I am today the only man in New England who can do it. I am perfectly happy and contented. Happy New Year."

CHAPTER 6

". . . the Walt Whitman of our painters."

Living with the sea almost at his front door, in the 1890s Homer devoted his painting to a new kind of subject—pure seascape. Up to this time his work had been basically figure paintings, although the sea had certainly played an important part. But from 1890 on, people began to play an increasingly lesser role, and the sea itself played an ever larger role. Homer's first pure seascape was *Sunlight on the Coast,* dated 1890, and was soon followed by his first winter subject in Maine, *Winter Coast.* We see the same kind of drama that Homer had expressed in his earlier pictures of men struggling against the sea. But now it is a purer, more elemental battle—the battle between the forces of sea and land. What interests Homer now is the eternal tension that exists between the furiously pounding surf on the one hand, and the quiet, monumental strength of the towering cliffs on the other.

Homer exhibited these two pictures, along with two others done in the same year, with his New York dealer in February 1891. A reviewer in a magazine called the *Collector* wrote: "To say that Mr. Winslow Homer exhibits at Reichard and Company's galleries the four most complete and powerful pictures he has painted, is to do them but half justice. They are, in their way, the four most powerful pictures that any man of our generation and people has painted. . . . A great American artist, in the full greatness of an art as truly American as its creator; what words could mean more?"

Homer painted fewer paintings in Maine than he had in his youth. He generally averaged about three finished pictures a year. Never interested in repeating himself in any way, he was constantly searching for new variations in light, atmosphere and weather. Sometimes he would leave a painting unfinished for months or even years, waiting for the exact effect of fog, or sunlight or cloud formation. His seascapes, although they may seem at first similar on the surface, never became routine products. Each one represents a different mood, a different approach and a new solution to a problem of light or weather. Extremely particular about his work, Homer refused to become simply a mass producer of standardized scenes. In late October 1892 he wrote: "I have painted very few things this summer, for the reason that good things are scarce and I cannot put out anything in my opinion bad."

Homer had two dealers during these years who exhibited and sold his paintings for him—Reichard and Company in New York, and Doll and Richards in Boston. Unlike most American artists of the time, Homer preferred to show his paintings at the galleries of his dealers than to exhibit them in the larger annual shows in New York's National Academy of Design. Perhaps he felt better suited personally to these smaller "one-man shows" than to the enormous, impersonal and overcrowded group exhibits. In any case, it seems to have been a wise decision from a financial standpoint. In little over a year (from January 1891 to April 1892), Reichard managed to sell five of Homer's eight new oil paintings. We can therefore understand why Homer wrote to Mattie in

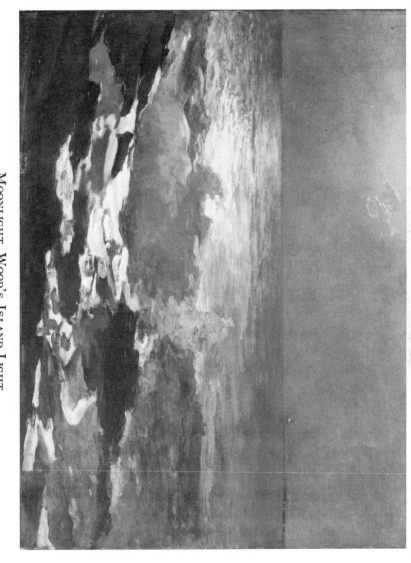

MOONLIGHT, WOOD'S ISLAND LIGHT
The Metropolitan Museum of Art
Gift of George A. Hearn, in memory of Arthur Hoppock Hearn, 1911

1892: "You will be glad to know that I have had great luck in this past year and as Father tells me, I am rich."

The New Yorkers who frequented Reichard's Gallery and who bought pictures by Homer were some of the most discerning collectors of the day. Among them were a few who had friendly personal relations with the artist and some who did not know him at all. Once, in 1891, Homer exhibited a large water color called *Mending Nets*. It was a picture he especially liked and considered one of his best. He therefore marked it with what he thought was a ridiculously high price, assuming no one would pay such an amount and he would be able to keep it for a while longer. Arriving at his brother's house after the opening of the show, he said, "Charlie, what do you think, some damn fool has gone and bought that picture." The "damn fool" was a man named Charles W. Gould, who later bought over twenty more pictures by Homer. (Today they are the prized possessions of the Chicago Art Institute.)

But by far, Homer's most dedicated patron and collector was a man from New York named Thomas Benedict Clarke. Although he had noticed Homer's work before, Clarke became seriously interested in Homer around 1890. Clarke was an unusual man and worlds apart from other active collectors of the time. In those days, all the American collectors were competing to see who could come back each year with more paintings from the Paris salon exhibitions. Nobody gave a second thought to purchasing American art and supporting American artists. Nobody, that is, but Thomas B. Clarke, who concentrated almost entirely on the works of native, living artists. He was never afraid to buy from young and unknown men, as well as from more recognized artists. And he never bought a picture he didn't like. But he must have liked quite a lot, for at one point the size of his collection was over four hundred paintings.

The artist Clarke liked the most was Winslow Homer. By the fall of 1891, when Clarke exhibited his collection in Philadelphia, he already had purchased twelve works by Homer, including the famous *Eight Bells*. During the next year, Clarke bought six more Homers, and followed with several others. He also began to persuade some of his rich friends to do the same. Homer was indeed fortunate to have captured the interest of such a wealthy and devoted patron. It has been said that next to Charles Homer, Clarke was the most important influence on the artist's life and career.

Early in 1892, Clarke wrote a letter to Homer at Prout's Neck. He said he had decided to devote an entire room in his house to Homer's work, and was going to call it the "Homer Gallery." The artist answered: "I never for a moment have forgotten you in connection with what success I have had in art. I am under the greatest obligation to you, and will never lose an opportunity of showing it. I shall always value any suggestion that you may make." Homer went on to say that Clarke should feel free to borrow any of his pictures at Reichard's to hang temporarily in his Homer Gallery.

Homer spent most of the next winter working on his largest and one of his best paintings, *The Fox Hunt*. It pictures a certain terrifying scene that occasionally takes place during the height of a Maine winter. At this time, when the ground has been frozen over with ice and snow for several weeks, a flock of starved crows would sometimes attack a lone fox. In Homer's picture we see the desperate animal trying to run through the deep snow, while overhead the menacing birds begin to descend on him. A cold winter sun slowly begins to break through the clouds, while in the distance the pounding waves break on snow-covered rocks.

Once again Homer has depicted a primitive struggle between two forces of nature. And he has done it beautifully and simply, with extraordinary power and impact. The painting is both realistic and decorative, showing three-dimensional space and at the same time creating a lovely pattern on the surface of the canvas. We might say that the picture is, in a sense, both simple and complicated. And how, we may ask, was such a powerful understatement of cruel drama actually put together?

The idea had been brewing in his mind for some time when Homer asked two of his neighbors, both excellent hunters, to bring him a dead fox and some dead crows. He arranged the dead fox, holding it with sticks and string, in a running position in the snow. The crows were then posed as if in flight on a snow drift outside his studio window. They were left outdoors overnight so they would be frozen stiff in the morning. Now, with everything carefully arranged in his composition, and with the shore visible in the background, Homer set to work painting. One of his neighbors later told how upset he became because "the weather keeps thawing and the crows get limp." After he had made some progress on the painting, Homer asked his friend Elbridge Oliver, the stationmaster, what he thought of it. "Hell, Win," his friend answered casually but frankly, "them ain't crows!" And Homer promptly painted out the crows.

Elbridge Oliver then suggested that Winslow come over by the station and spend some time watching how the crows flock over there. For three days they scattered corn on the ground around the outside of the station to lure in the crows. And for three days Homer made sketch after sketch on the backs of telegraph forms. When he was finally satisfied, he returned to his studio and painted the crows in their final version. Elbridge Oliver stopped by the studio the next day and gave his final approval, and Homer was at last pleased. Time and again we see that Homer was much more impressed with the criticism of his friends and family than with the elaborate reviews written by well-known art critics.

The Fox Hunt was exhibited at Doll and Richards' Gallery in Boston in 1893. The art critic for a Boston newspaper called it the most important painting by Homer he had yet seen. He went on to say: "There is something very impressive and solemn about this stern and frigid landscape, and it is a fit scene for the impending tragedy that threatened the fox. The painting of the drifted snow in the foreground is exceedingly interesting in the delicate gradations in the values on the undulating surface, in the delicacy of its color, which is apparently very simple yet is full of variety."

The next year *The Fox Hunt* was shown in the annual exhibition of the Pennsylvania Academy in Philadelphia. It was bought after the exhibition by the Pennsylvania Academy for $1,200. In the same year, 1894, *The Fog Warning,* which had been bought earlier by Homer's wealthy cousin Grenville Norcross, was donated by Norcross to the Boston Museum of Fine Arts. So, by 1894, Homer already had pictures in two of the country's largest public collections.

In 1895, three of Homer's seascapes were exhibited at the Pennsylvania Academy, and the critics' reviews were again full of raves. Homer had become, in his own lifetime, America's most famous and best-loved artist. The deep feelings of respect and admiration the public held for him are best summed up in a review that appeared in *Scribner's Magazine* after the Philadelphia show in 1895:

"Truly there is hope for a country that has produced a painter of such uncompromising honesty. . . . But Mr. Homer has other claims on our admiration than his independence: his Americanism, so pronounced that one might call him the Walt Whitman of our painters."

In February 1899, Thomas Clarke decided to sell at auction his entire collection of paintings. At this point his collection comprised 372 pictures by American artists, 31 of them by Winslow Homer. The largest and most important auction of American art to that date, it was of course attended with great excitement by the public and press. As each work was brought to view on the auction block, the enthusiastic audience greeted it with a round of applause. The bidding was high and resulted in American pictures being sold for new record prices. And the prices for Homer paintings were among the highest—$4,700 for *Eight Bells*, $4,500 for *The Life Line*, and $4,400 for *The Maine Coast*. Slightly higher amounts were paid for a few paintings by other artists, but the Homers gained the highest prices for works by living painters. Clarke, of course, was delighted with his profits, for he had originally paid sums as low as $400 for *Eight Bells* and $800 for *The Maine Coast*. (Some of Homer's best paintings are today valued at about $100,000.)

Looking at the Clarke sale from a financial point of view, we see that some significant changes had taken place by the end of the nineteenth century. Up until this time, it was generally felt that American art was secondary to European art (and therefore secondary in price). But the Clarke sale brought new record highs for American art. It was, in a way, a statement by the public that American art had finally "come of age." " 'Nativism' in art seems to have arrived," a New York critic wrote the day after the sale. Lloyd Goodrich, today's leading authority on Winslow Homer, has written: "The Clarke sale gave native painting the kind of prestige the American public respected most—that of dollars and cents."

Winslow Homer had spent that winter in Nassau, and wrote a letter to Clarke from Florida, where he was stopping on his return trip north.

"Owing to the delay in the mails I have only just received the news of the great success of your sale. I owe it to you to express to you my sincere thanks for the great benefit that I have received from your encouragement of my work and to congratulate you. . . . Only think of my being *alive* with a reputation (that you have made for me)."

CHAPTER 7

". . . it is certainly the richest field
for an artist that I have seen."

Soon after Homer had settled at Prout's Neck in the early 1880s, he took the first of several trips to the tropics. He sailed in December 1884 for the Bahamas, stopping in Nassau for about two months, and making side trips to the nearby islands of Eleuthera and Harbour Island. The Caribbean had not yet developed into the sea of tourist resorts that it is today. In fact, Winslow Homer was one of the first Americans to take regular vacations in this part of the world, and he certainly was one of the first artists to paint there.

When he arrived in the Bahamas, Homer was nearly stunned with what met his eyes. Everywhere he looked all that he saw was bathed in a bright tropical sunlight that he had never before seen. Having experienced sunlight only in the more temperate zones of North America, he would never have thought that such clarity and intensity were even within the realms of possibility. But here he was, standing in this almost blinding light, shocked and impressed in much the same way that Gauguin must have been when he first arrived on the Caribbean island of Martinique. This bright sunlight is an impressive sight to any tourist, but to the eyes of an artist it must be truly overwhelming.

THE GULF STREAM

The Metropolitan Museum of Art
Wolfe Fund, 1906

Adirondack Guide

Courtesy, Museum of Fine Arts, Boston
Bequest of Mrs. Alma H. Wadleigh

East Point, Prout's Neck

Sterling and Francine Clark Art Institute
Williamstown, Massachusetts

And the colors! We can imagine with what curiosity and interest the artist approached these new exotic colors and shades. The powerful light revealed incredible ranges of blues in the Gulf Stream waters. White limestone roads and houses seemed to sparkle in the sun. Homer was, of course, enormously pleased with the dazzling beauty of the lush vegetation that seemed to spring up almost everywhere. He spent day after day happily discovering for himself new varieties of tropical plants and flowers. We see in his paintings that he especially loved the coconut palm, the orange and grapefruit trees, the aloes and the frangipani with its bright red leaves.

Homer was fascinated with the appearance and activities of the black population of the Bahamas. Twenty years earlier, when he had covered the Civil War in the South for *Harper's Weekly,* the artist's eye had occasionally lingered on the local blacks. Even then Homer did not portray black people or plantation life as stereotyped conceptions. He always painted his subjects with a feeling of warmth and humanity and, above all, with dignity. Each subject was seen as an individual, not a cliché. Here in the tropics Homer viewed the black population diving for conches, chasing turtles along the beach or skillfully maneuvering fishing boats through dangerous waters. Their shining mahogany-colored bodies, with smooth skin tightly covering well-developed muscles, are always beautifully contrasted with the clearer tones of the white walls and blue water.

Here was another world, another aspect of nature for Homer to paint. And this is exactly what he did, producing a large quantity of pictures during the first three months of 1885. Homer again took up water-color painting, just as he had done when he had visited Tynemouth more than a decade earlier. A quicker, more fluid and more portable medium, water color was the perfect solution for the artist who was always on the move, often tenuously perched on an unsteady vehicle or boat.

Homer did not treat these water colors as preliminary sketches for large oil paintings. They were painted as end products in and of themselves. This was a radical departure from conventional attitudes toward the water-color medium —most people regarded water color as either a sketching medium or a simple pastime to occupy the idle hours of young ladies. In contrast with his Maine oil paintings, water color became the vehicle through which Homer expressed the warmer, more vibrant side of his character.

In the nineteenth century, water color was simply not thought of as a serious means of expression. It is largely through Winslow Homer's glorious group of water colors, done in the tropics during the last twenty-five years of his life, that this attitude began to change. Indications that the public was beginning to take water colors more seriously are seen in a review of Homer's first water-color show in Boston: "Mr. Homer goes as far as anyone has ever done in demonstrating the value of water color as a serious means of expressing dignified artistic impressions, and does it wholly in his own way."

Before his journey to the Caribbean, Winslow's brother Charles gave him a small, boxlike camera, probably an Eastman Kodak No. 1. Homer used this camera, and in subsequent years later models, to take several series of travel photographs. He would often paint a water color by basing its subject matter on the scene in a photograph. A comparison of any of his photographs with the similar painting provides us with interesting insights. The photograph remains as a visual record of a specific scene—it is an interesting pictorial document, but no more than this. The painting, on the other hand, is an example of how the artist eliminates nonessential details, distills light and shadows down to their basic elements and generally *selects* what he wants to accentuate. This element of selectivity is finally what underlies and distinguishes the art of the painter.

Winslow Homer was not the first American artist to become interested in photography as a corollary to his painting. Various artists had experimented with this medium ever since the first photograph, the daguerreotype, was invented in Paris in 1839. Samuel F. B. Morse, who was well known as a painter as well as an inventor, brought a daguerreotype apparatus back to America later that year and soon opened a photograph studio in the New York University Building in Washington Square. Frederic Remington, an American artist famous for his paintings of galloping horses, probably based his pictures on a series of photographs by Muybridge. And Thomas Eakins, a Philadelphia artist who lived during the same years as Winslow Homer, even went so far as to invent a very early version of the motion picture camera. This interest in scientific discovery and technology was common to many American artists of the nineteenth century.

The steamships that stopped at Nassau would continue on around to the east end of Cuba. After spending about two months in Nassau, Homer decided to take one of these steamships to the ancient Spanish city of Santiago de Cuba. Winslow found this place immensely interesting, but in a different way from Nassau. Situated on a gorgeous mountainous coast and overlooking a large harbor, this picturesque Spanish colonial city was a strange combination of an earlier grandeur and a present-day squalor. He wrote to Charles: "Here I am fixed for a month. . . . This is a redhot place full of soldiers. They have just condemned six men

to be shot for landing with arms, and from all accounts
they deserve it. The first day sketching I was ordered to
move on until the crowds dispersed. Now I have a pass from
the Mayor 'forbidding all agents to interfere with me when
following my profession.' I expect some fine things—it is
certainly the richest field for an artist that I have seen.
You talk very poor up North. Why do you not sell your
horses and buy one from Nassau for 60 that will beat any
that you have for going over the roads, they eat anything
they can get and have never seen an oat. Lucky Father did
not go with me. No breakfast until 11, very bad smells, no
drains, brick tiles and scorpions for floor and so hot that
you must change your clothes every afternoon. I will be
very glad to get home."

Many of Homer's Cuban water colors were views of the
city, showing its narrow streets and old Spanish houses. He
found these unusual architectural forms very appealing and
recorded them with his camera and with his brush. In a
large series of Santiago street scenes we see that the artist
was especially charmed by such picturesque features as the
richly textured stucco walls, the wrought iron grillwork on
the outsides of the houses, and the balconies and rooftops
drooping with hanging moss. The bright sunshine illuminated
these scenes in deep contrasts of light and shadow which
resulted in interesting abstract patterns in many of these
water colors.

The following January, 1886, Homer did travel with his
father, spending about a month fishing and painting in
Florida. They stayed in the region of St. John's River in the
northeast corner of the state, in one of those isolated backwoods areas that Homer always loved to find. Pictures of
men fishing and boating and a superb series of palm tree
studies characterize Homer's Florida water colors. In all

these pictures we see a new feeling for light—a clarity and luminosity that distinguish these works from the heavier, darker paintings done in the North.

The winter of 1903 to 1904 was again spent in Florida. Just before Homer sailed from New York to Key West, he wrote his brother Arthur: "I have an idea at present of doing some work but do not know how long that will last—at any rate I will once more have a good feed of goat flesh and smoke some good cigars and catch some red snappers." Homer was obviously in high spirits when he left for Florida, and his happy mood is captured in the series of water colors he did in Key West harbor showing fishing boats with their crews. Concentrating more than ever on the effects of light and color, Homer carefully selected the essentials in each composition—clear blue water and bright white boats contrasting dark brown bodies and gaily colored clothing.

After a few weeks in Key West, Homer moved on to Homosassa on the Gulf of Mexico, a spot well known for bass fishing. Here, when he was not busy landing a fish, Homer painted more water colors. Sometimes he would paint a life-size close-up of a fish leaping out of the water, its iridescent scales shining in the sunlight and reflecting in the water. Some of these brightly colored studies of fish are indeed masterpieces. They form a special chapter in that branch of American art that has been involved with the artistic investigation of natural species. Homer's studies of fish, in fact, rank with Audubon's birds and Heade's flowers as first-rate pictures in this category.

Although Homer had spent a happy and productive winter in the Caribbean in 1886, he did not return again until 1898, nearly fourteen years later. A good deal of his time during these years was occupied with caring for his aging

father, who died in 1898 at the age of eighty-nine. Homer
had lovingly watched over his father to the end, and soon
after his death he wrote to Thomas Clarke: "I am notifying
certain people who I may expect to hear from in the next
six months that I shall not be in Scarboro Maine." To another friend he wrote: "I go somewhere in the West Indies."

"Somewhere in the West Indies" turned out to be Nassau,
where he stayed and painted for three months. Homer's most
famous oil painting, *The Gulf Stream,* was a direct result of
this trip. He painted it in Maine several months later,
basing it on various water colors he had done in Nassau.
The idea for this painting must have been brewing for quite
a while, for, on his return trip north, Homer wrote to his
friend Clarke: "I have had a most successful winter in
Nassau. I have found what I wanted and have many things
to work up . . . that I have in mind."

The Gulf Stream is the last of Homer's great "perils of the
sea" subjects. It differs from the earlier ones in that it is a
tropical scene and therefore much brighter and more colorful than those of the Maine coast. But the same sense of
drama and danger, the same uncertainty of man's eternal battle with the sea are here in this picture. *The Gulf Stream* is a
painting of a black man adrift at sea in a sloop with a broken
mast. He is exhausted, nearing starvation, and is in grave
danger from the hungry sharks who circle menacingly
around his boat. The water is unusually choppy and rough,
causing the boat to tilt at a precarious angle, and a waterspout rising in the distance poses an additional threat to the
helpless man. Homer knew when he painted it that this was
one of his finest, most powerful works, and today *The Gulf
Stream* is the artist's best-known painting.

The director of the Pennsylvania Academy asked Homer
twice if he would exhibit *The Gulf Stream* at the Academy's

show opening in January 1900. Homer flatly refused—twice. He finally gave in at the last minute when he received a telegram saying: "The greatest American art exhibition cannot open without an example from the greatest American artist." The picture was hurriedly sent off to Philadelphia before it was actually finished, along with the following warning from the artist: "Don't let the public stick its nose into my picture."

When *The Gulf Stream* came back from Philadelphia, Homer continued to work on it for almost another year. He wrote to a friend in September: "I have painted on the picture since it was in Philadelphia and improved it very much (more of the Deep Sea water than before)." And finally handing it over to Knoedler, his new dealer in New York, Homer said: "Show it for all it's worth, in the window or out of it. . . . I had rather have a picture in your show window than any place."

Despite the fact that Homer considered *The Gulf Stream* his best painting, Knoedler wasn't able to sell it. The obstacle seemed to be the overly polite, refined and sentimental tastes of the public, who found the subject too gruesome and frightening. The Worcester Museum in Massachusetts, which at one point considered buying it, finally turned it down, apparently because of two lady trustees who found it "unpleasant." But before the ladies made their decision they asked Knoedler for an explanation of the subject.

Homer wrote to Knoedler in 1902: "You ask me for a full description of my picture of the Gulf Stream. I regret very much that I have painted a picture that requires any description. . . . I have crossed the Gulf Stream *ten* times and I should know something about it. . . . *They have been blown out to sea by a hurricane. . . .*" At another point the artist was even more annoyed when he wrote his dealer:

"The criticisms of the 'Gulf Stream' by old women and others are noted. You may inform these people that the Negro did not starve to death. He was not eaten by sharks. The waterspout did not hit him. And he was rescued by a passing ship which is not shown in the picture."

The Gulf Stream was shown several years later, in 1906, at the annual exhibition of the National Academy of Design in New York. At this point the public and critics were able to judge the picture with not quite so much Victorian sentimentality, and most agreed that this was indeed Homer's masterpiece. The Exhibition Jury recommended that the Metropolitan Museum purchase the picture, which the museum did without hesitation. And the critic for the *Evening Post* called *The Gulf Stream* "that rare thing in these days, a great dramatic picture, partly because the horror is suggested without a trace of sentimentality and partly because every object in the picture receives a sort of over-all emphasis that shows no favor to the dramatic passages. As a result the story never outweighs the artistic interest."

CHAPTER 8

". . . he usually caught the biggest fish."

Homer's love of traveling and the outdoors was not confined just to tropical climates. Beginning in 1889 and continuing almost every year until the end of his life, Winslow and Charles went on fishing trips in the northern backwoods country. From 1889 through 1894 they spent part of each summer in the Adirondacks, first at the clubhouse of the Adirondack Game Preserve Association, and then later at the North Woods Club near Minerva in Essex County. This was a densely forested and mountainous region of upper New York State, containing the tiny streams which make up the headwaters of the Hudson River. Much of the area was rough and uninhabited, and for the brothers it was a long ride by buckboard into the wilderness they loved.

Some of these trips were strictly for fishing, but more often Winslow would combine art and fishing, working quickly in water color as he did in the South. Next to painting, Winslow's favorite activity was fishing, a sport he faithfully pursued at home in Maine as well as during his travels. It appears that Winslow was just as talented a fisherman as he was an artist. His brother Charlie once said: "He did not go in for elaborate or expensive tackle, but he usually caught the biggest fish."

Homer chose his Adirondack subjects from the vast selection of natural settings and wild life that surrounded him. In these water colors we see the deep, cool greens of the forest contrasting the still, clear blue water. We see a picture of a deer drinking from a stream and can almost sense the quiet hush in the air. In a lovely painting called *The Mink Pond* we have an intimate, close-up view of a frog and other creatures floating among water lilies and pickerelweed, while a brilliantly shining fish flashes by in the crystalline water. Homer also painted several life-size pictures of trout leaping from the streams, just as he painted other fish in Florida and the Caribbean.

The most interesting of the Adirondack water colors, however, are those pictures in which Homer shows man together with nature. But these scenes differ from the man-in-nature paintings done in Maine and the South, for they reveal a more comfortable, harmonious relationship between the human figure and his surroundings. All seems perfectly well balanced and peaceful in these enchanting pictures of fishermen in canoes, men returning from hunting, woodsmen logging in the upper Hudson River, and sportsmen casting for fish above a waterfall. In these water colors we see that Homer has achieved a new breadth of vision. His eye and his brush are perfectly attuned to each other as he selects the essential details and merely suggests other forms and shapes through strong washes of color.

Winslow often began these water colors while in the Adirondacks, and then painted in the human figure after he returned to Prout's Neck. One of his most successful pictures, *Adirondack Guide,* was done exactly this way. Here, as in many other Adirondack scenes, we see a portrait of John Gatchell, Homer's occasional handyman and model in Prout's Neck. Gatchell, a bearded, lanky, weatherbeaten type, was a perfect substitute for the tough, old Adirondack guides.

THE MINK POND

Courtesy of the Fogg Art Museum, Harvard University

Grenville L. Winthrop Bequest

HOUND AND HUNTER
National Gallery of Art, Washington, D.C.
Gift of Stephen C. Clark, 1947

Homer had previously painted Gatchell in his well-known *Eight Bells,* and through the years this striking man became the artist's most popular model. Gatchell, the story goes, was a little too fond of alcohol, and so had trouble finding work to support his wife and seven sons. But Winslow felt sorry for him and tried to give him odd jobs whenever he could. This is typical of Homer's many kindnesses to the local folk around Prout's Neck. As his sister-in-law, Mattie, told one interviewer after Homer's death: "If you want to know Winslow, ask the poor people of Prout's Neck."

Homer's trips to the Adirondacks were the inspiration for two oil paintings. In October 1891, Winslow was busy fishing and painting in Essex County. Charles had just returned to New York from a European trip and received the following letter from his brother: "I am working very hard and will without doubt finish the two oil paintings that I commenced on Oct. 2nd and great works they are. Your eye being fresh from European pictures, great care is required to make you proud of your brother. The original ideas of these paintings are in water color and will not be put on the market, but will be presented to you with the one that I made expressly for you."

One of these two oils is *Hound and Hunter,* a picture of a young woodsman lying in the bottom of a boat, grabbing the antlers of a deer in the water. He is shouting to his hound to come to his aid. It is a powerfully realistic picture, showing the hunter in a natural and unheroic manner. We get an interesting insight into how carefully Homer observed the minute details of his subject in a comment he made several years later. Bryson Burroughs, another artist, told Homer how much he admired *Hound and Hunter.* "I am glad you like that picture," said Homer, "it's a good picture. Did you notice the boy's hands—all sunburnt; the wrists

somewhat sunburnt, but not as brown as the hands; and the
bit of forearm where the sleeve is pulled back not sunburnt
at all. That was hard to paint. I spent more than a week
painting those hands."

Winslow Homer never pretended to be modest about the
paintings he felt were good. Describing *Hound and Hunter*
in a letter to Thomas Clarke, he said proudly: "I think I
owe it to you to give you more particulars about this oil
picture. I have had it on hand over two seasons, and now it
promises to be very fine. It is a figure piece pure and simple,
and a figure piece well carried out is not a common affair."

Starting in 1893, Winslow and Charles began regular
trips to Quebec in search of fresh fishing and camping
grounds. They joined the Tourilli Fish and Game Club on
Lake Tourilli near St. Raymond. This was a completely
wild and isolated area of deep forests, miles away from any
settlement, and was reached only by a blazed trail. The
brothers had a log cabin built on the lake and for many
years spent part of each summer here. They would set out
on camping trips with canoes, supplies, and four or five
guides and spend weeks following the complicated network
of streams and lakes. Although both brothers prided themselves in being rugged sportsmen, Charles, at least, was aware
that he was getting on in years. "I want two guides in the
boat and one on the road," he wrote, "so that in traversing
the portages one man will be with me to repair damages as
my bones are getting brittle with age."

Winslow, on the other hand, was less apt to be daunted
by his age or the lack of comfort on these trips. On one
occasion Winslow went alone to Quebec in February and
settled at Roberval on the shore of Lake St. John, a big lake
more than a hundred miles north of Quebec City. The year
was 1896 and Homer was exactly sixty years old. We see

BEAR AND CANOE

Courtesy of The Brooklyn Museum

how insistent he was on maintaining the image of his own toughness and strength. He wrote to Charles: "The place suits me as if it were made for me by a kind of providence— but I pity any man who would expect to be satisfied by the accommodations he would find at the Island House at Roberval."

Roberval soon became one of the favorite haunts of the Homer brothers. It was the home of the famous ouananiche, or landlocked salmon, considered a formidable catch by even the most expert anglers. Winslow spent a good deal of time on Lake St. John trying his hand at catching these fearsome fish, but he always found time to paint as well. He painted many water colors in the area of Lake St. John, sometimes showing other anglers playing the fish, but more often scenes showing the life of the local Montagnais Indians. Homer, as we have seen, was always interested in painting people, particularly the local types of each area. Thus, we see that the protagonists of his Prout's Neck pictures are the local New England town folk, the central figures in his West Indies scenes are the native blacks, and in Quebec he was fascinated by the Indians.

The site at Roberval was reached by a difficult canoe trip up the treacherous Saguenay River. Steep rocky cliffs surround the Saguenay, which flows for miles through gorges with protruding rocks and turbulent rapids. Only the most expert canoeists were able to navigate such a trip. We can well imagine how Winslow must have loved this wild, majestic aspect of nature, just as he thrived on the violent storms along the coast of Maine. He apparently was so enthralled with the Saguenay River that he would make the river trip more than once or twice a summer, always trying to capture the thrill of this experience in paint.

His favorite subjects here were, of course, the French-

Canadian and Indian woodsmen as they skillfully maneu-
vered their primitive canoes through the raging foam. In
these scenes he found the same tense drama of man against
nature that had fascinated him all through his life. On one
occasion Homer paid a guide ten dollars to shoot the rapids
so that he could sketch the man from the shore. The guide
agreed, the transaction was made, and Homer stayed on the
shore waiting for the canoe to come careening by. He waited
and waited and finally when his patience had run out he returned to camp to see what had happened to the guide.
Winslow found him casually sitting there and demanded to
know why he had not appeared shooting the rapids. "Mr.
Charles paid me ten dollars not to," the guide answered with
a perfectly straight face. Perhaps he did not realize that this
was another example of the fun these brothers always had
playing jokes on each other.

These Quebec trips resulted in an oil painting, *Shooting
the Rapids, Saguenay River,* dated 1905. Although the
painting was never finished, it remains one of Homer's most
masterful studies of man's relationship to nature. The story
connected with the conception of this work is an amusing
example of how Winslow enjoyed himself by poking fun at
his brother. On their first visit to Lake St. John the brothers
had hired the services of four very capable guides. To show
their appreciation near the end of the trip, the Homers gave
each of the guides a pint of whiskey. But the foresighted
guides had no intention of letting the bottles break or spill
during the rough downstream canoe trip. Drinking the entire
contents on the spot, the guides drunkenly prepared to de-
part, and placed one of the Homer brothers in the center of
each canoe. For years afterward both Winslow and Charlie
talked about this memorable journey down the Saguenay,
with four drunken guides wildly paddling through the turbu-

lent rapids. Although both brothers were no doubt equally nervous, Winslow later took the opportunity to record the scene as he viewed it. The picture shows Charles sitting low in the canoe, hanging onto the gunwales for dear life. Winslow certainly chuckled to himself as he painted the expression of utter panic on Charlie's face!

SHOOTING THE RAPIDS, SAGUENAY RIVER
The Metropolitan Museum of Art
Gift of Charles S. Homer, 1911

CHAPTER 9

"Football, Thanksgiving and other things
will make no difference.
This is the best place."

One of the proudest moments in Homer's life came during
the summer of 1900 while he was back in the Adirondacks.
He received a letter from Mattie saying that he had been
one of the artists to win gold medals for his paintings shown
at the World's Fair in Paris that year. (Charles, too, had won
a medal for his brilliant research in chemistry.) The French
Ministry of Fine Arts was so impressed with Homer's picture
A Summer Night that they decided to buy it for the Luxembourg Palace Museum in Paris. Homer had painted this picture ten years earlier in Prout's Neck. It shows two girls danc-
ing on the beach at night, silhouetted against the sparkling,
moonlit waves.

The artist had always valued this particular work and was
more than a little pleased that it met with such success in
France. Homer, after all, was one of the few American artists
who had not been trained in Europe, and it made him happy
to know that he could nonetheless satisfy the high artistic de-
mands of the French. And imagine how pleased Homer
would have been if he had known that France's most illustri-
ous artist at that time, Claude Monet, was one of his ardent
admirers. An American critic had met Monet and asked him

what he thought about American painting. Monet spoke highly of Winslow Homer, this critic wrote, "whom he knew and admired through the painter's nocturne in the Luxembourg." (*A Summer Night* is still in Paris and can be seen at the Musée National d'Art Moderne.) Toward the end of his life Homer won many medals and prizes, but the one he valued the most was this gold medal from Paris. He apparently kept it in the breast pocket of his pajamas during his final illness.

Homer began the last decade of his life in 1900 at the age of sixty-four. He continued to stay alone at Prout's Neck into the winters, and continued to love the coast of Maine as much as ever. He paid great attention to caring for the large share of land his father had left him—building houses, fences, and roads and selling lots. He spent more and more time with his old friends, the local, year-round residents of Prout's Neck. Still valuing the artistic criticisms of these honest people, he would often invite one of them in for a drink, a smoke and conversation. There are numerous stories about how Homer could not stand the criticisms of out-of-town visitors and often refused to let them enter his studio. But just as often he would invite in his butcher when he made his meat delivery, talk with him for an hour and let him "tear his pictures all to pieces."

Homer's fondness for Prout's Neck never diminished, even after he was there for more than twenty years. He wrote to Charles one autumn: "You have no idea how fine it is here for me. The sun is low and shines in across my floor all day in my two living rooms. Only think of all the room here with plenty to interest me. I shall stay here until the snow is four inches deep. Then get out. Football, Thanksgiving and other things will make no difference. This is the best place."

One morning early in the summer of 1908, Homer appeared at his brother Arthur's cottage, complaining: "I don't know what's the matter with me. I have been two hours getting dressed and getting over here." He complained of dizziness and it was obvious that something was also wrong with his eyesight. When he reached for his teacup at breakfast, Arthur noticed that Winslow missed it by several inches. Arthur immediately called the doctor, who declared that Homer had suffered a slight paralytic stroke. Resting in Arthur's house for two weeks, Winslow's strength soon came back, and with it his desire to be active and on the move again. A few days later he wrote to Charles, with obvious relief and pleasure: "I can paint as well as ever. I think my pictures better for having one eye in the pot and one in the chimney. A new departure in the art world."

Despite his illness and weak condition, Winslow insisted on leaving a few days later for the Adirondacks. From his old haunt at the North Woods Club he wrote touchingly to Charles: "I appear to be very well. There is only one thing I do not understand about my recent illness, that is, that I cannot tie my neck tie in the way that I have done for the past 20 years. It is impossible for me to make that sailor's knot. Every four or five days I try to do it but as yet it has been of no use trying. As you see, I now can write plain enough, and in all other matters everything is all right. Try and find out what was the matter with me."

Homer returned to Maine in late July and insisted on staying on alone into the winter. Although he now looked much older and moved more slowly, some of his old strength had returned. He had not done much painting for a few years, and had occasionally even announced that he had given it up for good. But now, after his illness, his creative drive returned and he wrote to Charles around Thanksgiving that he had found something interesting to work on, and that this suited

him much better than sitting around loafing. Perhaps refer-
ring to the mysterious complexities of this creative impulse
that had just resurfaced, he added: "There is certainly some
strange power that has some overlook on me and directing my
life." A month later he was still at work on the same picture.
"I am painting when it is light enough on a most surprising
picture but the days are short and sometimes very dark."

The "surprising picture" is Homer's striking duck-hunting
scene called *Right and Left*. (This is the hunter's term for
knocking down a bird with a shot from each barrel of a
double-barreled gun.) It was to be one of his last oil paintings. A fascinating story is connected with how Homer
actually conceived the idea for this painting. His friend
Phineas W. Sprague of Boston, a summer resident of the
Neck, had decided to stay on that year for the autumn duck-
hunting season. One day in November Sprague bagged some
ducks and left a brace of them hanging on Homer's door—
probably a present for Thanksgiving. Immediately upon seeing them, Homer's imagination was fired up and he decided to paint a picture of ducks being shot. In order to
study the subject in his typically thorough manner, Homer
hired a local hunter, Will Googins, to take him out in a boat.
Day after day he sketched the scene from different angles,
always studying the varying effects of the gun blasts and the
stricken birds. When he finally put it down on canvas, he
was once again able to distill all his different studies into one
perfect composition. Instead of showing the ducks as they
would have been seen from the vantage point of the hunter
in his boat, they are close-ups, yet obviously seen from far out
over the water. It is as if the artist has gone up in a heli-
copter, entering the space occupied by the ducks and viewing
them head-on at the moment they are shot. In the distance
we see the vaguest suggestion of a hunter in his boat, and,

because we are close to the ducks, we can almost feel the shattering violence of the impact. The extraordinary point of view taken here, as well as the stark simplicity of the design, make *Right and Left* one of Homer's most powerful pictures.

Some of the most tragic yet fascinating chapters in the history of the New England coast involve the stories of shipwrecks. Homer's last water color, painted about 1908, was based on an actual shipwreck he had witnessed five years earlier from the cliffs of Prout's Neck. Although he simply titled the work *The Wrecked Schooner,* it has been positively identified as the wreck of the *Washington B. Thomas.* This legendary ship was built at the Watts shipyard in Thomaston, Maine, and was launched on its maiden voyage to Norfolk in April 1903. All those involved with the building of the *Thomas* had high hopes for her success, despite the fact that wooden schooners were beginning to be threatened by competition from metal steamships. The *Washington B. Thomas* was built as a superschooner and was meant to answer the challenge of this new competition.

To insure the success of this superschooner, its owners hired a well-known and respected master, Captain William J. Lermond, to sail the ship to Norfolk for a lucrative cargo of coal. Captain Lermond invested his entire life's savings by buying one third of the coal himself, in order to sell it in New England and make a large profit. On its return voyage to Portland harbor, the *Thomas* was forced to stop in a dense fog near Stratton's Island, about six miles from Prout's Neck. During the night an incredibly violent storm arose at sea. The ship was torn from its anchors and was mercilessly dashed upon the jagged rocks of Stratton's Island. Before the night was over, the *Thomas* was battered to pieces, the shipment of coal was lost, and Captain Lermond's young bride was drowned. The captain himself died a few years later, a broken and impoverished man, in Sailors' Snug Harbor, Staten Island, New York's home for destitute seamen.

Homer was clearly moved by this tragedy, and made several sketches of the remains of the schooner in the next few days after the fog had lifted. *The Wrecked Schooner,* according to Mattie, was the last water color Homer completed. In many ways we can regard this as a fitting conclusion to the artist's long years of studying the perils of the sea. Significantly, there are no human figures in this picture—just the wrecked schooner, the sea and the rocks. As he became old and feeble and weaker in the face of nature, Homer no doubt began to realize the real meaning behind the theme of man against nature—the theme that had preoccupied him for most of his life. Perhaps this painting was Winslow Homer's final recognition in old age of nature's ultimate power over man.

THE WRECKED SCHOONER
The St. Louis Art Museum

CHAPTER 10

"All is lovely outside my house
and inside of my house and myself."

In the summer of 1910, Homer began to suffer from a painful stomach ailment. His ill health was apparent to everyone around him, but Homer refused to recognize it himself. He wrote the phrase "I am very well" repeatedly in his letters, and insisted to his family and friends that he was "all right." But when William Macbeth, the New York art dealer, came to visit him at Prout's Neck that August, he noticed the seriousness of Homer's condition.

"What proved to be his last illness had already laid its grip upon him," Macbeth later wrote, "but in spite of pain he insisted on giving himself to me, and together we roamed over his Prout's Neck possessions, with their many wonderful views, far and near. He found an excuse for going to the farthest point in order to cut out some branches of shrubbery where insects were playing havoc on the grounds of one of his tenants. . . . 'From this point I painted *The Fox Hunt*,' and so on, pointing to the scene of many a familiar canvas. . . . He knew that his work was over."

And indeed it was. Winslow Homer died on the afternoon of September 29, 1910, at Prout's Neck, with both his brothers by his side. He was seventy-four. He was buried in Mount Auburn Cemetery in Cambridge, Massachusetts, alongside his parents. Nearby were the graves of Longfellow, Holmes, Lowell and many other New Englanders who—like Winslow Homer—have made rich and lasting contributions to America's culture.

Homer was admired and respected in his own time for many of the same reasons he is today. He was one of those unusually rare occurrences in history, a self-taught artistic genius. Homer developed his own personal style, his own means of expression, paying no attention to "accepted" styles or tastes. His independence is all the more remarkable when we realize that most artists at that time studied in Europe and tried to imitate fashionable European styles. Homer lived in Maine, turning his back on fashion and style. He did not choose to compete with other painters working within certain dictated modes that were essentially alien to his own experience. He painted the world as he saw it, not some romantic, make-believe world based on history or mythology. Honesty and truth were his guidelines, resulting in an art that is basically and supremely American. Winslow Homer was, in a very real sense, our first truly American artist.

Winslow Homer was born in 1836, when America was still a young and struggling country. But when he died in 1910 his country had entered the twentieth century and in just a few years would become a modern and powerful force among nations. During his lifetime Homer witnessed America's growth from a basically rural, agricultural society into a country of crowded urban centers filled with masses of newly arrived immigrants. The Gold Rush of 1849 had opened the western frontier, and networks of railroads were beginning to tie this massive continent together. And almost every year, it seemed, science and technology were producing startling new inventions—the steam engine, the sewing machine, the automobile, steel-beamed skyscrapers. Winslow Homer saw all this happening—he was a witness to the Industrial Revolution. A witness, but not a participant.

Homer's move to Prout's Neck coincides almost exactly with America's sudden and enormous industrial growth. For this artist, basically a simple and serious man, the crowded, noisy, active city life no longer answered his needs. Not that he disliked people—we have seen this to be quite the contrary. But he was that rare kind of artist who got inspiration not from other people but from solitude. His work always came first. Sometimes for days on end he was so busy painting that he didn't talk to another person. This kind of commitment is unusual, and perhaps explains why Homer never married. He was, after all, married to his work.

Homer's preoccupation with the elemental forces of nature was, no doubt, a reaction against the rapid changes going on in the world around him. He had a basic love of nature in her unspoiled aspects, a nostalgia for the natural face of America as opposed to the man-made face of America. And through this love Homer has preserved for us today a picture of our country's original, unspoiled natural beauty. It is a healthy, energetic picture, filled with movement and mood, but rarely based on personal feelings. Homer's view of nature was almost always objective and resulted in a truthful, unsentimental realism. Like the man himself, his art is direct and strong.

A sense of poetry exists in Homer's paintings. His pictures are visual poems dedicated to that important side of our national character—our love of physical adventure in the wilds of nature. Melville, Crane and Hemingway are among the writers who have praised this same aspect of American life. No painter has done it more successfully than Winslow Homer. His vision was clear and uncompromising, based on a simple relationship between himself and his surroundings.

Writing Mattie two years before he died, Homer summed up his own philosophy in his usually succinct and unassuming manner: "All is lovely outside my house and inside of my house and myself."

Linda Hyman, a native of Buffalo, attended Vassar College for two years before she went on to Columbia University for her B.A. and M.A. in art history. For many years she was on the staff of The Metropolitan Museum of Art. She lives in New York City, where she is a lecturer on American Art at the City University of New York.

Courtesy of the Pennsylvania Academy of the Fine Arts